GERRY CAMBRIDGE was born of I
twenties he worked as a freelance i
and as a journalist for numerous
photographic press, the house m
Reader's Digest. For 25 years he
Ayrshire before moving to Hugh MacDiarmid's cottage,
Brownsbank, near Biggar, South Lanarkshire, from 1997-1999
as the Brownsbank Writing Fellow. In the mid-1990s he
founded, and still edits, the Scottish-American poetry
magazine, *The Dark Horse.* As an essayist on poetry, he has
contributed to both the *British Writers* and *American Writers*
series published by Charles Scribner's Sons in the U.S., and to
the *Oxford Encyclopaedia of American Literature.* A frequent
visiting writer to schools across Scotland, in mid-2002 he was
the poet-in-residence at Lawthorn Primary School, a mile from
where, for a quarter of a century, he put down roots. As a
blues harmonica player, with the singer-songwriter Findlay
Napier, Cambridge has performed at venues including "T in
the Park" and on BBC Radio Scotland. He plays session
harmonica on blues singer Linda Jaxson's CD *Not Guilty* and
on Scottish folk musician Neil Macdonald Thomson's CD
Common Ground. Two of Cambridge's poems, 'The Nature
of Burns' and 'Madame Fi Fi's Farewell', have been put to
music by Thomson and performed at venues across Scotland.

By the same author:

The Dark Gift & Other Poems (St. Inan's Press, 1994)
The Shell House (Scottish Cultural Press, 1995)
"Nothing But Heather!": Scottish Nature in Poems,
Photographs and Prose (Luath Press, 1999)
The Praise of Swans (Shoestring Press, 2000)

Dot.

Saw this guy live at a poetry
evening organised by my
mate Mike. He played blues
on the harmonica & enthralled us
with the simple magic of his
words. Scotland, & women,
what more can a man write
about. ü Wumble

Madame Fi Fi's Farewell
And Other Poems

GERRY CAMBRIDGE

Luath Press Limited
EDINBURGH

www.luath.co.uk

First published 2003

The paper used in this book is neutral-sized and
recyclable, though it is hoped that the latter fact will not
be taken as a suggestion. It is made from
elemental chlorine free pulps sourced from renewable
forests.

The publisher acknowledges subsidy from

Scottish
Arts Council

towards the publication of this volume

Printed by IBT Global, London and New York

Typeset in 10.5 Sabon by
Dark Horse Typesetting

For My Mother and Father

ACKNOWLEDGEMENTS

The author wishes to thank the editors of the following publications, in which poems from this collection have appeared: *Back To the Light: New Glasgow Poems* (Mariscat Press/Glasgow City Council, 2001); *Mr Burns for Supper* (Greit Bogill, 1996); *The Ice Horses* (Scottish Cultural Press, 1996); *Across the Water: Irishness in Modern Scottish Writing* (Argyll Publishing, 2000); *Dream State: The New Scottish Poets*, 2nd edition (Polygon, 2002); *The Independent*; *The Herald*; *The Spectator*; *New Writing Scotland 13*; *New Writing Scotland 14*; *Norman MacCaig at Eighty* (Chapman Commemorative Book); *Sparrow, the Yearbook of the Sonnet*, nos. 61 and 62 (U.S.A.); *Lines Review*; *Southfields*; *Janus* (U.S.A.); *The Formalist* (U.S.A.).

'The Absence of Letters' won the Sonnet Prize in *Sparrow* 61; 'Adolescent Bodybuilders' appeared on *Cutting Teeth* 9, a limited edition CD version of the magazine, with the author's own harmonica accompaniment; 'Candles' was the Glasgow Underground poem for February 2000; '1%' appeared in *Profile, Full Face* (The Van Zora Press, Massachusetts, 2001); '13 Ways of Looking at Edwin Morgan' was written for *Unknown is Best*, a celebration of Edwin Morgan at Eighty (Mariscat/Scottish Poetry Library, April 2000); 'Island Letter' appeared in the 'British' issue of *The Hudson Review* (New York) in Winter 2000, which included the author as one of eight contemporary British poets. Some of the poems in Section II first appeared in the chapbook *The Praise of Swans* (Shoestring Press, 2000), which is now out of print. The poem 'Water' was used for the English CYSY Paper III in Practical Criticism in 2002 by the Scottish Qualifications Authority.

CONTENTS

SECTION II

AUTHOR'S NOTES

"SOMEONE ONCE REMARKED that poetry has a built in lie detector. By the time you come to write the stuff with any force, you are more or less fixed in your own character and personality. You may envy so and so for their shapelier nose, or their greater affluence, or their sexier body, poetically speaking, but you have to make do with your own portion of eternity."

—From: *One Piece of a Triptych*

"I SENT AWAY for a bodybuilding course entitled, with absurd optimism, *Hercules II*. The £12 cost of this I earned by a weekend of hoisting hay bales at local Fairliecrevoch Farm. This added considerably more muscle than the three month course itself which, advocating that I consume enormous amounts of protein, served only to outrage my thrift-minded father and enlarge my girth. Alarmed by the latter, I became near anorexic in reaction. This was buttressed by my pleasing sense of sanctity when I learned that, at a certain stage of self-starvation, my sex-drive almost disappeared. I could then view my female classmates less with alarming lust than with a lofty and pseudo-innocent regard. Sex was a sin, after all. So eating had to be a sin, too, for eating led to sex. And sin, though it was how we were all here in the first place, was indisputably bad. I grew thin as a stick, but felt holy..."

—From: *From the Irish*

"SOMETIMES, SITTING, he would think: *I've been waiting for something to happen to me all my life. I've been waiting for some sort of visionary experience, that would change everything about me, and give me courage and poise, and let me behave sinlessly.* To behave sinlessly! As if that was possible! Every mouthful he ate was taken from the mouth of a starving child, he knew, and because he was alive someone else could not be. He remembered how as a little boy he would say to himself, 'I will count to ten, and when I reach ten, everything will be different. I will make a completely new start.' And he would count to ten, and begin."

—From: *The Story of Bill Porter*

I

1%

My conversation's ninety-nine percent
poetry, you complain; and the last percent is sex.
As partners go, I'm hardly heaven-sent:
outdated as *Tyrannosaurus rex* —

if less well-armoured. Lust and verse
is certainly a threadbare repertoire;
and I'm obsessive. I must improve: rehearse
my knowledge of tectonics and the Loire,

bone up on Scottish Kings and Queens,
The War of Independence and the French
Revolution, Trinidad's cuisines,
and the natural histories of the perch and tench.

Less talk in smooth pentameters, or raving on
your slimline ankles, knees, or inner thighs.
I'll learn the proper use of words like 'paragon';
I'll teach you the genetics of fruit flies.

On things like this I will become expert,
though they, of course, seem less to do with you.
I'll silently admire your hands or shapely skirt.
One percent, I think, is not quite true.

The Absence of Letters

I must choose life, and it is here with you
When with a hair-tossed flourish, and all bare,
You take on its stand the candle and walk through
Dark rooms to the unlit bathroom, where we
Like figures from some medieval mystery
Take a hot bath together, whispering, aware
As here we are wreathed in perfumed steam,
Of the whipping night outside and the long scream
Of the gale. There's nothing else to be satisfied
After our hours together, except we be
Cleansed and calmed and, fragrant, dried,
Then wrapped in dreamless sleep. And suddenly
Poor Yeats, you say, *besotted with Maud Gonne!*
All those letters! Between us, hardly one.

The Dark Gift

Pure white and buff flight feather, tawny owl's.
I found it by the lane as I walked home,
kept it for your interested son, its comb
and furriness, despite his adolescent scowls
and rancour, fascinating. I used to search
far woods round here, confused teenager, for
lush primaries of those birds I rarely saw,
on mornings when my mother thought the church

contained me. Tonight you drive me back
up the Glasgow road towards the city's
knives and angers, all the human pities
and our own. Dazzling road signs mark the black.
And you hit the wheel, as I clutch this tawny's feather,
as we speed on through the autumn night together.

Praying Mantis

Found in Andalucía's autumn night
on the road between red blossoms to the sea,
and caught by my thrown shirt, insect Nefertiti,
Egyptian queen, dazed from looping flight
about the streetlamps. I carried her unhurt
back to show your sons.
Fresh leaf-green, hypnotic-graceful; female,
we supposed.

We watched how she'd begin
to clean herself fastidiously — then pause,
to turn a triangular, high-cheekboned face
to look with eerie grace at me or you
across the room. Those spined front arms!
Gently-working jaws.

Then she'd come to, and clean herself again,
upslanting, over all our heads,
up on her curtain rail, as you harangued
your sons over unwashed dishes, unmade beds;
silent as we all stormed about and banged,
and ignorant of children, women, men.

From Spain

For you this pomegranate, the 'love apple'
as you told me, wary lest I would present
it to some other woman, not knowing what that meant.
Sonnet of an assuaging globe. A chapel
packed with its ruby congregation, your
small white hands will liberate to the air
and light, loosen the shining crowds with care,
and heap on our washed plate. Before,
here in a frosty Scotland, minds away
from its Andalucían hillside, and the day
you watched me pick it, in those hot uplands,
winter deepens, open its perishing richness, seeded, sweet.
I bring it on your birthday, for your hands.
Worship's end: world-round, red-tinged, complete.

Body Song

Your lipstick smudges pink my white cup-rims.
Pale thighs below long dresses that you wear,
Deft fingers at my undoing, and your red-fierce hair,
Shatter my old existence, and its hymns.

These hothouse days are all a case of glands.
Oh sacrifice me, apply your lipstick slowly,
Burn me to pure body that alone is holy,
A willing victim under your white hands.

The body's the thing that can never lie.
Pretence is mind's respectability
Which cannot win again here, though it try,
And I pretend to prefer, now far away,
That girl, too-pure as a showery noon in May,
Who walked on Overtoun, morning and night with me.

A Gift

Your mouth's red horse has galloped down
the generations; so many men
it's carried off, as me again
to the dark sea where we all drown,

glad. Or it's an ominous key
unlocks the world's door I step through
to where the vital acts accrue
to time's last tick for you and me.

Your mouth's my courage; lacking this,
how should I dare the devious world?
Your mouth is every flag unfurled,
that act's root is each promised kiss.

And that kiss is the sun of guilt
lighting me through every day;
toppling into act each *may*,
there's no strong house, that lacks it, built.

Adolescent Bodybuilders

Hercules II! I clipped the little ad
and sent for it. Twelve quid. Then once a week
each posted part proclaimed: *A dynamite physique
in just three months!*
                              It's naethin but a fad
my father mocked.
                              I understand why, here,
surrounded by your weight-bulged adolescents
posturing and preening like cock pheasants.
Muscles! Mirrors! Gasps! And the top cock's fear.

Five nights a week, bedroomed, I'd heave and strain.

*What better than your woman being thrilled
by your large biceps and your superb build?*
Hercules enquired.
                              Nothing, I knew,
examining my stick-frame for each gain.

Twenty years it took to get the woman too.

Ditty

O, Miss Aphrodite Saltcoats
  Is the girl for me,
She makes most men get out their boats
  And sail upon the sea.

She paints her nails, shapely, long,
  In delicatest shade of pink,
And laughs, and sings a little song
  Of men who cannot think:

O Aphrodite, I am done
  With thought, the finest say;
Let us retire to eat the sun,
  And fold away the day;

Many a room, through you, is bare,
  And many a tear is shed,
Started by that flesh you wear,
  And many a heart in dread.

O Aphrodite, Aphrodite,
  Take your silk blouse off for me:
I'll stop being high and mighty,
  Nor venture on the sea.

The First

Sue Donaldson! She had what is called *it*.
Men buzzed like nervous bees when she was near.
Wordless, she electrified the atmosphere
in sea-green frock, as she would sit,
her legs demurely crossed, and sip hot coffee.

A neighbour. She was my introduction
to woman's otherness and dreamt seduction,
and I the light that couldn't escape her gravity.

My frame unfilled, a bumbling adolescent,
silk-minded, I hoped the marvel would occur
as I searched woods for nests — that I'd find her,
far from the smoky living room's covert looks.
There, her nearness charged my circuits incandescent.
And I plunged deeper into my nature books.

Obsession

The A. A. Book of British Birds. I'd got
the latin names of all those birds by heart
at fifteen, and showing off would start
reciting. And I was proud knowing what
nidifugous, nidicolous, meant, in all weathers
tramping Cunninghamhead, delighted when I saw
verified, a dead heron's pectinated claw
one evening as I searched for eggs and feathers.

Oh neo-Wordsworth! Nidicolous youth!
Each May I could have told where a hundred nests were.
I knew where every summer migrant went.
Strix aluco I repeated, mantra for the truth.

Sue Donaldson passed me in a dwam of scent.
I never found a latin name for her.

Elegy
23 December 1995

Sue Donaldson, I want to praise
beyond your death your earthly days:
struck down by a heart attack
at fifty, you'd the knack
in nineteen seventy-four or -five
of making all connections live,
of trembling adolescent knees,
and buzzed male brains like nests of bees
wild for fleshly honey. Oh,
your air that made testosterone flow
I never, teenaged, understood,
except it seemed a terrible good
when near. It was your aura filled
my head when youth's life over-spilled —
messy, and uncontainable.

You were my village sybil.
You'd wave to me when washing up
each ordinary plate and cup:
below your sweater your full breasts
dreamt hot as eggs in thrushes' nests,
your cleansing sudsy hands that, wet,
you dried to smoke a cigarette,
were centre of my teenage thought
barbed-wired round with *must* and *ought*.

Sheer fantasy! That time you beckoned
by rapping on your pane a second,
crooking a finger in your living room
as I walked past, how not assume

that it meant my seduction? I
knocked your open door to die.
You rustled in the bedroom, said
I'll be out soon. My birling head
rushed with blood that reeled my frame
bayed by dogs of lust and shame.
And all you wanted was a hand
to shift a couch, common, bland —
no strawberries and double cream
of my half-nightmare and half-dream.
You twenty-nine and I fifteen,
of course you couldn't set a scene
in which I gave my all.
      Your last
lover wipes away the past,
utterly strips you down, alone,
to smallest stitch and simple bone,
and fills with earth the subtle mouth
that made my adolescent south —
where you still walk, so sexual there,
though vanished from our daily air,
whom no man any more may see
except in mortal memory
live and smiling in blue dress,
front-buttoning, from happiness.

The Queen of the Night
"I will paint my toenails deep purple..."

The Queen of the Night
is men's downfall,
and men's delight.
Her toenails laquered deep
purple rouse in sleep
men in their married beds,
and solitary men, appal
the priest with his desire,
and stir, in old men's heads,
the flicker of a fire.

Down through humid dark
she moves, smudging her scarlet mark
on the white or the brown skin,
offering the shining lips
and the brand of fingertips
letting the fresh world in,
promising her salty creams
to the poor perfected dreams,
opening her fiery earth
into a further birth;

out of the tall sun
down through the grove of night
for absolute wishes, she
troubles them all undone,
smelling of apples, blood, the sea,
as men's downfall,
and men's delight.

Epigram

Safe settled love is weeping at Eros,
That daimon who rhymes imperfectly with loss.

Lady's-smock

I

You picked these lilac wildflowers from the lush
grass that grows like a jungle, rain and sun-fed
here, that I'd to mow; arranged them, spread,
in a white cup on the table; I want to crush
their delicacy, it's almost unbearable, how light
cherishes against the enamel's white
the tremulous lilac blossoms and slim green stems
as thought of your bare skin under your dresses' hems,
the gold down of your thighs, your wisps of flame
that are for my eyes only, and your name
that puffs out in blossom on blossom on my lips
when I die in your earth and self-hood breaks
and we flow together, and you are the god who takes
the most of me with mouth and thighs and fingertips.

II

The phone is answered, and you come to speak,
who should have stopped this months ago,
inconsequent talk of mine; you must know
all is, between us, done. But we're both weak.
Passivity now I understand's a crime
unrecognised, and ours fashioned this day
I wake in, startled, a year, a life away;
yet I still, proprietorial, waste your time.
No fire in the flint when struck appeared from you.
Passivity stopped your anger searing through,

and stops it still, which was our end, old crone
passivity. Here how the wildflowers burn
in hedge and ditch, and active guilts return
but don't prevent. Curse me, down the telephone.

Blood Root

There had to be only one in that
archipelago of tables, free —
it had to be next to yours.
As soon as I noticed you, the old
conspiracy of walls moved in, the hot
tributaries overflowed
their banks of *may* and *should* and *not*
and flooded my blanked-out head.
You had your back to me, its thin
white nylon sweater showed the straps
of your bra and the small sweet knobble
where they joined for the unfastening
and the blossoming of roses in our mouths,
the absolute liberties of skin
on skin. Had you then turned and looked,
would you have seen the blood I need
to be rid of, that sings to be drunk
and gone? In the gloomed
wood of that gaze,
my happiness at half-
measures, half-solutions,
and all the ordered syllables of light I built are lost.

In the Supermarket

That wouldn't be Wendy Anderson, would it?
    There, at the check-out queue.
Don't talk for a moment, please, while I try to fit
    An older face to a new.

(At least in a manner of speaking.) Yes, it is, I am sure!
    But her eyes nearly scuppered in folds of fat,
And her bottom's wobbling inheritance no longer the lure
    For boys who'd gape for the blue 'V's glimpse when she sat.

She's noticed me, and her look, as if she has guessed
    Says, *What's that bald skinny guy gawping at?*
Suddenly the strands of my hair feel messed.
    And I forgot my hat.

A Whitmanian Reply

for David Kinloch, after his sestina

Hearing you read out your poems on a dreich night in
       Glasgow, making the CCA a centre of the whole
       pubbed riotous city,
writing of poets who turned back in fear from the open
       Whitmanian road to sonnets of such insignificance
       not even a microscope shows them,
I thought: *let him away with that? Never! Carnaptious
       and havering scunner!*
O where are the modern free versers with a droplet of
       Whitman's rhythmical energy,
rhythm that's the root of the universe, with metre its
       regular partner;
or of the orbic flex of his balls, singing the paean testicular,
       jetting his love-juice abundantly over the umbrella'd
       masses
detumescent and muttering curses?

Chopped prose, and I say — what is that?
Meanings obscurest to all but the most intimate friends —
       what are they?
I say I have more in common with Whitman than any free-
       verser, in a time of sonnets he wrote rhythmical free
       verse based on the prose in the Bible,
in a time of free verse based not, alas, on Biblical prose I
       write sonnets, quatrains, and some ballads.

I sing of the forms wholehearted and sensual, I sound my
       chirruping invite over the lipsticks of the world.
Hearty, eating and drinking, if you want me again look for
       me among the suspenders.

Amphibrach, dimeter, caesura and pæon, I lie and loaf at
     my ease among the prosodic textbooks, all of which
     I ignore.

Cunninghamhead is as much a centre as Glasgow,
my cat has come in with the chill of the whole Universe on
     her fur, maiowing for food,
the Pleaides sparkle in the autumn night through the clear
     skylight in the roof of my caravan, the dole has just
     sent me a summoning letter —
I tramp through the puddles to sign on,
Mr Cambridge, a young girl says, with a minister's thumb
     at the base of her neck,
will you go on a training scheme, we have lots of places,
     (plenty of chances for drowning in paper,
and all of small meaning in our fudged-up bureaucracy)?
Christ, I'm a writer of sonnets I say, and writing loads now,
     and I say that to be a writer of sonnets is noble,
and that there is little greater than a writer of sharp clean
     sonnets.

Song

"I'll tell you of my evening with a youth
from Aruba, whose tan I could feel in the dark."
                    —GM

Let me tell of my night with a youth from Aruba
   Whose tan I could feel in the dark;
His flesh was as tight and as smooth as a tuba —
   On it I left my mark.

I picked him up in a local dive,
   That glossy and sleek, Aruban youth;
Half to prove to myself I was still alive,
   And half to ease love's drouth.

He had the need and I the apartment, so
   Why the hell not? I said to myself;
A youth from Aruba like this one will go.
   I'm tired of sitting like a vase on a shelf.

So back we went, for lust's advent;
   The din of our labours woke the whole block
But made worthwhile my extortionate rent.
   Oh I enjoyed it, till a thought like a rock

Brought a face more distant and stark
   As after I lay with my youth from Aruba
   Whose flesh was as smooth and tight as a tuba,
And whose chill I could feel in the dark.

Old Man in the Department Store

Gun points of lipsticks in their serried rows
protrude. And gladly I'd surrender
among the boudoir splendour
to the force I never chose.

Mauve, scarlet, brown, pink, red —
young I fought them, zipped up, tight;
who gave up briefly every night
by day played the stiff saint, instead.

And now, beyond attacks, I see
their thrilling armies everywhere.
Bright-mouthed and with such tossed-back hair,
they'd have no task subduing me.

On a Young Librarian

Frost's poems, this being Scotland, in reserve,
you have to fetch them for me, go off, down
and far, as I imagine it, through brown
shelves of sleeping books, your every curve
and colour marvellous among the dust
and angularity, searching for a master's
life-monument to joys and to disasters,
a spectrum gathered from white light's lust.

You've found them, and come breathless, red-
cheeked from that dark place, your wrap
slipped off one bare shoulder as if you'd fled
back up to peopled warmth and kinder lands,
poems of Frost contained — oh that bra strap
sliding down an arm! — by your white hands.

Lines to Another Emily

I sense as I sit close that you're aware of me,
who notice your neck's slenderness, too frail.
You're a watercolour, bone-china vase, and pale
as a bare page still to be written on. See,
my large strong hands are like birds, restless. We
spark such opposites, you and me; my blood-heat
blazes here in my red-bearded face; neat,
you sit like the form for a sonnet, whitely.

Watch me. I am the gale you lock your door to
that nightlong tests your buttressed walls.
I am the life you fear and lust for, charged and new,
that roars in the woods at your silent calls;
force to break through your charmed ring, and enter
to touch to glad sorrow in your dark centre.

Valentine Note

Love cannot be demanded,
But must be freely given,
And giving's circumstances
Are certainly mysterious;
Therefore the comeliest face
May light no twisted passion
Though many would expect it,
And lover make the quite
Unanticipated choice—
Except there's little chosen
Where love's entwined with sight,
For love's our plain astonishment
And heart guards its own
Reasons from the lover,
Never to be known.

Postscript to Love

Love: an arrangement of facial bones,
Or a small cheek scar from a biking fall
Prompting unexpectedly a kiss; a certain look;
A particular way of reading from a book.

And the acts of love are pitiless:
Its wine is vinegar in other mouths.
It burns the settled house to a waste of stones,
And its star will make the night in which to shine.

Madame Fi Fi's Farewell

*"Madame Fi Fi regrets to announce due to lack
of public demand she will shut her doors on Saturday."*
                                        —advertisement

Rattle down the shutters, cast away the key,
Relinquish the rivers at last to the sea,
   Old Jock of Lochranza,
   Taut as a stanza,
 Can come no more for me.

My eager sole visitor was planted this week,
Six decades beyond his potency's peak;
   He was the salty, last
   Proof of my glorious past;
 From here, the sea looks bleak.

It's out with the pension, no more red heels
To clack down the pier among wet nets and creels;
   I can't turn a head
   (When they are all dead)
 From the sea's late purples and steels.

Hang up my whip, my scents, the tools of my trade,
That kept the fish-scaled men unstaid;
   From the tedium of wintered lives,
   Beyond the scowls of island wives,
 Released them, glad-afraid.

Young men of Lamlash, Blackwaterfoot, Corrie,
Be you built like a rabbit, a shark, or a lorry,
   It's off with this make-up
   That let your dads wake up,
  And I am sorry.

II

Bus Journey in Snow

The snow-clogged wipers creaked on, back and forth,
their rhythm dull as Sisyphus's plod,
or an old gravedigger's spadefuls. God,
the teeming billions out of the whole sky, North.

" 's no real!" the driver cursed. The bus bumped,
and all our comic jetsam of full bags, and faces
as we wiped steamy windows, besieged by Baltic spaces,
swayed and lurched; three dozen backsides jumped
in time to the bus's moves, and smoking-red-as-hell
the driver, paid to be in charge, threw a curse
at the black mercurial Universe
as I thought of the mothers all round setting out tea
in the hot, lit kitchens while the crazy feathers fell
like confetti on stepped-out heads, or into the Irish Sea.

Irvine

A Winter Morning

At age 14, Ayrshire

Puddle ice cracked like lightbulb glass.
Frost had furred the last of the hips and haws.
My breath plumed out like a dragon's
In the cheering cold that morning the class
Was off for the day as the heating had failed —
Off for the week, with luck.

It was a gift, an escape from the wise laws
That governed things, a glimpse
Of possibility, like the thought
Of seeing a waxwing in an Irvine garden,
Or discovering a girl who liked you,
Or waking to find tremendous snow.
Not the escape itself, but its fine surprise.

Water

I venture out at midnight
for water at an outside tap,
my bucket and my kettle
light as air. How the clouds
have vanished and the moon
and constellations
shine up there, an audience
in jewels and hush
gazing from the balconies. Orion
and the fainter Pleiades,
the Plough directly overhead;
nothing between all these
and upturned face but space,
clear billions of empty miles.
The moon and its dead seas
are sharp within my eye. Here
the water drums into the bucket, its
sound altering as it fills.
With heaviness in left hand
and in right, careful lest it spills,
under the bright
amphitheatre, I
trudge back to a square
of light, its room lined
with workings of the mind,
with lingual astronomies,
closing the door
on the simple night.

From Cunninghamhead

That sudden rainbow, why, its foot appears,
from this door, as if planted in Kilmaurs —
that ordinary village — though physic's laws
deny it; still its bow, shock-clear
and hugely arched above the emerald woods
that tinily stir against the black-bright, looks —
as my eyes follow its curve from this room's books —
anchored in that main street with its goods
in shops, its pubs, churchtower. I'll cycle there,
and as the equivalent of a pot of gold
this afternoon, find in that street's air,
its ruddy faces, gutter leaves, shop windows,
the absolute earthly end of all rainbows,
as that street drips and dazzles in the cold.

Wasp at a Skylight Window

The wasp against the wide
  Conundrum of the glass,
Its wings a birring blur
  As upside down it tries
The smooth, transparent face,
Exhausts itself inside
  Before white clouds that pass;
Unable to defer
  To anything but the sky's
Promise of breezy space,
  Devotion is its doom:
  It cannot leave, of course,
This hopeful, dazzling source,
  And dare the darker room —
Its duller pane left wide
  To sheer tall miles outside.

The Day's Response
"It all depends upon your point of view..."
for William Neill

To answer you, here's been a big wild day,
With sudden glooms, and rattling showers, and then
Returning dazzle, all the restive trees
Glittering on black cloud miles East, and here
Blue air, and such pure white ferociously
Upwisped clouds around, above the woods,
And far off to forever. Each time I threw
The door of this small room wide open, far
Beeches roared in frantic crowds around,
And closer was a stand of sitka spruce,
The boughs of each arranged against the sky
Like wagging fingers pointing up in opposite
Directions to the air, while eastward a big flock
Of rooks against black cloud, in air uptossed,
Made blown soot in croaking whirls with sunlight
Glinting on dark wings, exuberant
Participants in the stadium of the day,
Under the sun and the travelling clouds,
Under the blue of space.   You know last year
I spent two months on Papa Westray, and
Was nearly driven mad. It was too real,
Too actual, bare stone, and rapid clouds,
Sun's high cataclysm and the wind that swept
From nowhere to nowhere, space, space, as if
A door had been flung open and I found
Myself stood at the edge of some abyss,
Naked to gusty brilliance. And every day,
Walking down the only road, I passed

A cow with single eye, its other just
A hole, a socket, ring of bone, the flesh
Around it swollen, so the cow's brow bulged
In deference to this god of stone that dealt
Its bangs to such softness. There were nesting terns
In thousands near the croft, and summerlong
And through each twilit night I heard outside
The blade-clash of their uproar, summoning
The day. And I remember when they left
Again, I noticed suddenly the vast
Stillness and hairst quietness there, the sea
Cobalt, the wave-crests sparkling white, with those
Clean clouds like clumps of pearls ranged round, far out
To horizons. A mile down in the bay
A lobster boat shone sharp and red, as if
Just newly painted, and now and then the road
Held a walker, tiny, yet giving a scale
To that tall sky. And, crowning all, such
Strange silence, as, far down below
While I stood at the croft door among docks,
From east shore spits the lagging terns uprose,
Lit small and sharp and brilliant white, like flakes
Of snow upflurried by an unknown hand
Against the cobalt sea, in all that air.
It was something vast, momentous, beyond
All theories, indisputable, the real,
Like now when I went out for water through
A countryside that dripped its night applause
Following sudden rain, the world a still-wet painting
Startlingly clear, where curlews called far up,
And yews were silhouettes against dark blue,
With scraps of constellations in the cloud-gaps
Refulgent in the rinsed height of the sky.

Gale

for Sam Gilliland

It was so windy, I joked at your door,
On my bike, I said, with a nod to northwards,
I arced over Warwickdale Hill like a rainbow,
Disdaining the road. We laughed. Nature's enormous show
That day — huge bright bow on black cloud, ash tree
High on a hill-top and shock-lit white, leaves
Skittering, panicked, away down the road,
Shower-squalls gone like giants, miles
In minutes, soaking and rattling faces elsewhere, you
Stood at your door, grey hair twirling
Down like corkscrews, Arran smudged
By squalls out westward, angling beams
As a man will spill an armful of sticks:
All seemed strange. Nature, eldritch,
Lifted my hair in each pounce round corners;
Lit with laughter, our eyes met;
Though we said nothing, acknowledged the music.

At the edge of the village, hilarious air!

Singing Bird

Christ's sake, poor Septimus, stop all this praise.
You make me seem a vase in some museum.
Goodbye the living poet, hello the mausoleum!
I haven't written an unselfconscious phrase
since you phoned in the small hours, raving
about my last sent verses, lyrical
sparrows daftly denying the empirical
hawk and its usual method of behaving.

I cannot write a word now but I visualise
myself an object, in your aesthetic gallery
of plinth-set poets, caretaken for a salary,
whose golden dung brings tears to aesthetes' eyes.
I'm out into the day to let the rain
batter me back to dailiness again.

Island Letter
to William Neill

From rain the sun this afternoon intensifies
Here to sudden brilliance, to surprise
This tablecloth checked red and white,
These scattered pens and papers, to delight
The mind with fresh untouched simplicity.
When I lean forward, look, down there I see
Papay's baby relative, the Holm,
Shine like an emerald in the bay, high foam
Making its slow uprise and silent fall
As usual on its east cliff, as curlews call
In the fast-cloud-shadowed field before
This pane.
     But I should tell you more
Just now about the croft I'm in; Tom Mackay,
Needing help, lets me it for nothing, and I try
My hand at haywork in return; its floor
Is of stone flags, its walls whitewashed, the door
Paint-cracked and peeling. And from the startled gaze
The cobalt ocean leaps, as ships on their various ways
Enlarge and pass, or drop beyond that edge
That looks to us a clean sharp ledge,
But to them unfolds landfall and ports and faces,
The constant emotions, the different places.

People, not things, are precious here: down
The west shore gravel track is the crown
Of earthly endeavour, kirkyard that I love
Reading epitaphs in, being briefly above
The dead's omnipotent helplessness: each name,

Harcus, Brett and Isbister, by the final fame
Of time, eaten by lichen. That startles here,
Out in light and breeze, where the west's clear
Three thousand miles to Canada, and I stand,
A tiny head in space, bootsoles on the island,
On the long brief journey of the beating heart.
But what I meant to get to at the start
Was how the sense of the island islands, also,
Time; each human encounter you can see in the glow
Of transience, in the hardworking now.
The island makes that possible, somehow;
No wonder the marvel of *The Tempest* Shakespeare set
On an island; they have that quality, yet.

And doubly that applies to tattie-bringing Tom Mackay,
(*Nat Gad*, as he would say, to my reply
To his question, *Then hoo groo thum?*
An dis that mean you doan't waant sum?)
Who brings them, free, in a bucket slung
Over his tractor's exhaust pipe; and dung,
And hay, and all the island's smells
Intermingle when Tom strides in, and tells
Me in his finest deadpan style,
No gleam in his eyes, nor three-toothed smile,
Whey, there's nuthin thee day ti celebrate, man!
You're still an this small island, an'
Why you shood waant ti stay here I doan't know.
Bluddy hell, if I were yung, I'd go
Aff in a meenat! And he'll sit a while,
And twirl his thumbs in the croft's silence, smile
Occasionally at something I have said
And speak of his old grandparents, long since dead,
As if they still lived in this small croft, and he

Was a bairn again, not yet bound on the sea
That's the end of hope for his life, but still walked
Into this croft where they often talked
Of the island's daily happenings, magnified
To that significance Kavanagh knew, inside
The commonest occasions. His tatties are
Magnificent, dense and nutty, and though they're star-
And rain- and soil-prompted, I agree
He *planted* them. He laughs with me.
Truculent, plain-speaking, one day he took an hour
To drive a mile, as the tractor kept on losing power;
You doan't seem too bathered by me trubble,
He announced from a mouth lost in stubble,
And we laughed in the island evening, calm
And vastly silent, the sound pewter-gleaming, balm
To the mind's red hours. Beyond Muir's myth,
Under the searing sun, I've helped Tom with
His hay work, sweated, drunk homebrew, woke stiff,
Felt real beyond the decoyings of *if*.
He is a fine man and I like him greatly, won't
Bow to the promptings of the Brethren here, who don't
Do anything Tom would have, could he have had
As he would say, *suffeeshant appartunity*. It's sad,
Hearing them loudly in their Gospel Hall
Sing grim hymns of punishment when all
The airy island evening's bright,
And silver's dancing on the sea, and light
Pours from the sun's fierce coin; they stand,
Larkin's 'death-suited', with, in hand,
The grief-black tomes, in the evening after;
Who trade, for eternal dullness, time's wild laughter.
But I can bear no grudges; the Rendalls asked
Did I need extra blankets when I was tasked

On my arrival by nights of unseasonal cold;
Perhaps their belief is new, their actions old.
At Clestrain, Gowrie's nearest croft,
Live Stewart and Isabel Groat, Stewart soft-
Spoken, a silver-haired old man who sits each day
Beside an Atlantic window or who may,
Walking-sticked, attempt the field behind.
His placed words issue from a full mind,
You feel. And Isabel, who sits and drops
In silence's pool when the talk stops:
We didna notice your gas lamp last night,
And when the ripples halt I say, "That's right,"
But nothing more, and Stewart, gray-eyed, smiles
As the late sun up in the placeless miles
Starts making a silver track on the sea through the pane
For the day's turned graceful now the early rain
Has stopped. What is a life spent only here
I think, far from the south's brutalities and fear,
White clucking sunlit chickens round the door,
Or days and nights of mist and the sea's roar
With the seals moaning from the east shore's skerry
To this old couple, who called me *Cherry*
In a Christmas card last year? I cannot say.

There is one shop, two churches, eighty folk here
Year-round, and tourists that with terns appear
Primarily in the long light; and one eight seat
Island plane that often tries to beat
Its record of under a minute from Westray
For the world's shortest flight, and every day
But Sunday, the mainland's ferry at the quay,
And events like Tom Mackay who stopped to tell me,
There's a package doon there fer yoo, and yoo owe

A canseederable sum fer its been lyin; "I'll go
Right now and get it; will it be much, d'you think?"*Oa,*
Maybe as much as a pownd; in a blink
I'll tek you. And we go.
                                   And, Willie, what
Real darkness can be like I had forgot
Till I came here, and walked by accident one night
Down some dirt-track that, with not even starlight,
I'd mistaken for the road. Or, approaching Gowrie,
To see it loom, star-perched, above me,
And to have to come inside and grope around
Among spoons and chairs and pens before I found
The lantern and the matches, send my shadow
Up the wall with the match's strike, before the glow
Of the lantern gave the room to me again —
Is to know more truly that the world of women and men
Is nothing to nature's ooriness, see that light
Is addition to the universal night,
Addition, and the night the root,
The *primum mobile* and absolute,
Or so I say just now. So I've taken,
Not trusting to what mind's fancies could awaken,
To leaving the lamp and the matches just inside
The front door, and to leaving it and the inner wide
To the miles of sea-breathed dark till I've made sure
There's nothing within to meet me. Pure
Imagination some would say, and yet
Although no townlife-softened type, if I forget
To leave the lantern handy my nape-hairs
Uprise, lest I be taken unawares.
But now the sun is out and warms my hands;
And all around today throughout the islands
Islanders make hay and drink home-brew,

As I on finishing these light lines will do,
For here comes Tom Mackay to fetch me now;
Will I look back in years to come, imagine how
Happy I was this day, and think it all a dream?
On the cobalt waves the crests are white as cream,
And Tom's here, straws for tractor seat, and he
In a panic to get the bales in. The boundless sea
Surrounds us, Willie, and I'll step on
To the box on the back of the tractor and be gone
From this small trade of versing and its joys
With Tom and his huge hands and his tractor's noise
Through the sweltering island day for miles
To hay bales and home brew and faces and their smiles.

Gowrie
Papa Westray
Orkney Islands

Duck Shooters

Out on the Overtoun Road in the autumn night,
Night of slow showers and the moon a blur,
Immense, calm, prospective night, my thoughts
On you I've hurt, and her; a shower
Stops, and the night world drips, and a veil now
Of cloud drags clear of the constant Plough
Over the dark farmhouse; look, it glints complete,
And star-patterns skinkle around the sky. At Warwickdale
The two duck shooters give me a lift;
I'm in a suddenly different world in the car's back seat,
And the two dark simple heads are framed
On the headlit road beyond. And all is warm
And comfortable, like a deep lulling dream,
Out of the threat of shower and storm;
They were shooting, they say, at Fairliecrevoch, and
Got nine duck — *three mallard, aye, six teal.*
Three mallard, and six teal!
I think of the spirits of air and dark
In the bags, their feathers superbly marked:
Bottle-green heads, cream eye-flashed, emerald specula,
And the wings that counties flowed below: three mallard,
        and six teal —
The eldritch, pristine real
In a jumble as if they were merely asleep
With their eyes now closed, in the bags!

Ye winchin yet? a voice asks. *Oh, on and off,*
I say. *I've just come now from a stormy session.*
Dinny let it get ye beat, says a different voice
An existence away; *ye'll no get oany stranger piece*
O chemistry than a wumman. It's thirty years' experience

Ah speak fae. They drop me off at the lane end; again
Sudden wide starlit sky, and above black trees,
The cloud-surrounded full and brilliant moon's
Bore down on by a cloud; the end of words.
And the door of the car
Slams, and tail-lights like red eyes it drives
Diminishing off down the empty road
Certainly, with men and guns, and dark-bagged birds.

Old Countryman

Willie Black — your beard as white as Venus in the dusk,
Or as the snowdrops in February's blasts —
With your finely-engraved Beretta, elegant server of death,
Leaning on the seat beside you
In the van on the Overtoun Road,
You suit this place, as I do.

Autumn in Ayrshire and all the trees hissing
      as if in excitement
In blustery dusks, lets you go off and be lost to yourself
Solid and strong, in what asks nothing.
The beautiful Universe here,
Shock-wet, late-sun splashed, hail falling smoky
      over miles of fields
Grants you perspective and balance.

An anthology of days of this small piece of country
Both of us love, you hold in your white-wisped head;
With such red cheeks
As if you'd stepped out of a story,
All that you wanted was your piece of eternity
Unchanged under sun and moon;
But, Willie Black, hunters are out for you and for me;
You scowl when you see
Their lights at evening, encampment of an army advancing

Against seasons and flood pools and skies.
No point cursing it, man,
Though curse you do,
While you rattle down rain-swept roads in your
    builder's van.

This Morning

Justin plays with light from space
  That catches his gold watch's gleam.
  He angles that trout-rapid beam
With a flick from cup, to wall, to face.

Eight minutes, ray, from sun to here
  You sped across the airless dark,
  Unborn until your brilliant mark
And welcome in our atmosphere

From one brown boy who toys with you
  Arriving, now, as minutes pass.
  Pure energy through common glass,
Griefless, and forever new.

A Fire in Winter

The owner cut the row of saplings back
one January, and one afternoon piled tall
once-flourishing boughs, and torched them all
as a chill dusk smoked in. Each burst and crack
later drew me out to the fire's life, from words
to gaze at summer's shade grown winter's heat,
the brawl of boughs being reduced to neat
manageable ash, as the winter's birds,
fieldfare and redwing, with their cries
flew overhead in darkness through the sky's
enormous anonymity. That blaze roared dry-red
face and wintered mind until to the dark's
swabbing effortless cool I turned instead —
Springside children's shouts, far exclamation marks.

Cunninghamhead Estate

Canticles for a Little Book

The mist that crept in here and stayed
as summer hangs flecked apples up
has hung with microscopic drops and made
visible
webs in hundreds
of tiny money spiders
in the field below this room;
see, in the gloom
of dusk, the pewter, silent webs
in silence, unconcealed
by their clear fruit so delicately slung.

***

Considering the yellowed sun,
I think of how
that distant furnace, though
mellowed by remoteness, here ignites
its fires at the backs of eyes;
and gazing in this small mirror, see
how yearly more prominent, cracked veins now
reflect in my cheeks
that roar in the dark complexities
of days; threshing, bound in me
what must, inexorable, win
back to its brilliant origin.

***

After an Image in Homer

The crab apple tree
back down the lane has come to fruition.
That abundant heavy condition
weighting each bough
with the green worlds, I envy:
for here and now
knives would be all such fruiting in me.

* * *

An Unwritten Page

That sheet of pure white
bisected by sunlight
in this little room
into equal triangles,
one shadowed, one bright
this squalled afternoon
(half the world moneying,
and half the world burned)
when I next look
is more shadowed than bright —

earth has turned

* * *

Small gates of the eye
  admit the bright sky;
and small words said
  boil in the head;
delight in the spring
  will know ripest sorrowing;
the summer's loud red
  in the frost will be dead.

* * *

As the hen redpoll
may these poems be —
  her intricate grams
safely a-sway
  in the topmost twigs
of a tall birch tree
on her clutch of five, and far
above the destined lambs.
  Not out of mind
of the herrying boy I used to be,
  but boughs beyond his touch.

* * *

Passing *The Goldberry* in the winter night
on impulse I throw the door open and look inside:
how the faces glance up in surprise and mild fright! —
from the various glasses where the sun's concentration
may burn out or focus the thought that everything passes;
that beautiful full-mouthed girl;
that grim man taking stock.

For a moment I feel like an artist, feel
love and a tenderness for
these souls in their box of time,
as if this were a painting turned back to its subject;
closing the door again
I step out in the cold
to the faces that pass like planets
under the night-hidden
gold of the Laigh Kirk's clock.

Kilmarnock

Letter to Timothy Murphy

Some lines to you in Habbie stanza,
A wee taut daft extravaganza,
Lubricated by three canza
    Scottish beer-O;
Slug such here, and any man's a
    Brief mad hero!

I'm pleased to see your verses, poet
Of certain gift and graced to know it,
For lacking that, you cannot grow it,
    Regardless;
No matter how you dung or hoe it,
    Growth will not bless.

Your *Sunset At the Getty*'s fine.
In fact I'd almost wish it mine,
So taut and spare in word and line,
    Clean-flowing;
Dark poem of all pomp's decline —
    The end of sowing!

No art without such knowledge can
Matter a damn to thinking man
Whether in farm or caravan,
    That is all one;
That knowledged edge is better than
    Bland chirping on.

Your mind is fogged with the barley-bree?
Frankly, it's the same for me.
The luminous masters' verses flee
        The whiskied brain-box;
Preparation for the threnody
        Of the stopped clocks.

Bunnahabhain and *Black Label*
Cowp poets in below the table,
Gift them with the tongues of Babel,
        Ranting, loud;
Yet doubly — though barely able
        To stand up — proud!

Whisky, grief's companion, came
To stake its visionary claim
And show the limits of Earth-fame
        In pickled brains;
That roof, nor page, nor face, nor name
        In time remains.

The world's a larach at the last,
All splendour's true iconoclast,
Open to the gutting blast
        And constellations;
Each future's seed its waiting past,
        And silenced nations.

But what of that, we've verse to make
Through city ruin and earthquake
For little but the making's sake
    When all is said:
So down with gloom, the old heartbreak,
    For verse is bread!

Your syntax punches on the nose,
While mine jouks to avoid such blows,
Not "strained" — your word — though far from prose,
    As I admit;
Though often with this poem's flows
    I score a hit!

I want my poems to all be knock-outs,
Oases in a land of droughts,
Bright axe-strokes in my mind of doubts,
    As Murphy's are;
But ach, my own conviction shouts
    Its thrawn exemplar!

Hell, I'll have to leave that style to you,
Be to my complex syntax true
As world is full of many a hue,
    Forby black/white;
As the world's ship has a motley crew,
    So poets write.

Yet this raised glass to wish you, there
Across three thousand miles of air
In those sight-losing vistas, where
    Your each verse ploughs,
Good whisky, poems, no despair —
    And happy sows.

A Note on Roy Campbell's 'Autumn'

Head over heart, he thought it bliss, himself alive,
seeing "all forms of life and feeling" die
"Save what is pure and will survive."
Therefore he liked against the winter sky

the fundamental black of twig and bough —
no messy leaves. Is that green bounty
less pure for annual withering, somehow?
Is it but a green deceit, over the winter county?

If winter is "the paragon of art",
sand-grain is better it would seem than pearl.
Yet here's a rigour, not of mind, but heart:
who'd ever prefer a skeleton to its girl?

Brownsbank Poems

I. *October*

Lecherous autumn undoes the gown of summer now,
stripping the papery leaves from the sycamore,
and backgarden cherries from their wind-shaken bough.
A startled blackie bumps the Brownsbank pane,
the light is watery and cold. It's a snell wind blows
the curled-up rowan leaves on the inscribed stone at the
      door
where moss in the letters of 'The Little White Rose'
presages the knowledge in 'The Eemis Stane.'

II. *December*

I step out for logs to the woodshed,
the stars beyond my dram-lit head
at their winking conversations...
How the whisky brings back things...
that girl whom I don't now know,
her tears ... thoughts of reconciliations —
craziness — with former friends...

There's Orion, over the black hills.
Pull open the door of the shed.
Logs.
      Birch, pine, elm, beech
in a heap, stark in the torch beam.
I pick the most solid in reach
thinking: *one or two summers ago*
these boughs held up the rustling seas
of starry green. I pile them

high in the basket and come inside,
pick a big one and throw it on the greeshoch
to sparks and the sudden lick
of flames. Then settle in the chair
suddenly wondering — *out there*
across the Universe, what beings
sit around what hearth-fires?

III. *Beside the A702*
Near Candymill

This winter-exposed nest
cushioned a redpoll's breast.
In topmost twigs of green
the hen and eggs have been
concealed beside this road
where lorries of heavy load
have thundered on their way
in dozens each spring day.
Their backdraughts must have made
her nervy as they swayed
and bounced that nest across
white clouds as if to toss
both eggs and her away.
How did she manage to stay
lodged in the hair-lined cup
while the twigs lashed, up
and down? I want to think she did,
forming a feathered lid
and bracing with bent-frail legs
above her frailer eggs.

IV. *8 a.m.*

The Lanarkshire hills are white with a frost
like dust that all night silently fell
from starry hammerwork. And strands of gossamer,
invisible yesterday, now hang from the fence,
frail chains, in their coats of rime.
When I go out for post to the box at the door,
in Brownsbank's porch, the inside panes, embossed
with the cold craftsmanship of night
weep for joy at the sight of the blooded sun.

V. *December Night*

Under the distant moon's cold light
the shed that MacDiarmid wrote in answers white
to the white of that dark-sea'd satellite;
under each leafless sycamore bough,
out for logs I shiver, noticing how
that shed gleams white as a moon-room now.

VI. *Near Christmas*

There's something delightful about this light in snow
this morning that gladdens the spirit
when logically it should be low,
a sense that's like the surprise
of poetry, its unpredictable freshness
not to be contained. I will go
down into Biggar where faces and eyes
I think will reflect the same sense
that no one of course will express,
and the shops be transformed by snow.

VII. *Solstice*
i.m. Valda Trevlyn
21 December 1998

I recall the dyed tint of Valda's hair —
the hue of that sun out there,
now nature's only fire, its ray
in all this pastel green and gray
attempting to melt the dust of frost
from the lines on the doorstep slab now mossed.
Something of her is that sun today.

Tale of a Cat

I didn't want her at first, not liking cats,
Takers of the birds that in hundreds in the spring set the
      woods
Astir with song, set the branches uttering green;
But one night in March when I opened the door of
      the kitchen
To stars and the beech hedge rattling with last year's
      leaves,
There she shivered in the track of light
Springing across the grass.

She fled into dark when I went out to fetch or to chase her;
I wasn't sure which.
Next day the cat-loving neighbours out on this hilltop
Were dropping their hints about kindness of cat-keeping;
I scowled from my catless paradise.

Next, though, she was curled near my step
In the March sunlight;
When I went outside she was rubbing herself on my ankle,
Tottered on weak legs,
Spine like string-pearls under my hand,
Tail thin as a rat's tail, and she leaf-frail, leaf-tremulous,
Atom
Under the sky;
I grunted, and opened a tin of sardines,
The spines infolded like silvery chains.

And so that began it. I tried to adapt to the new charge,
Though now and again, nights after, fantasised that
I took her out under the unclouded moon
(Her head bobbing in my arms as she wondered
        where she was going)
Set her in the centre of a field
As Handsel and Gretel once were set in the dark forest,
And ran away, and left her.

I didn't want this life.
I didn't want this life.
But back she would come, scratching at the door, as
        a steel nib scratches a page,
Wanting only to be taken in and kept,
Saying, if not in words, I am life, I am life, accept, accept.
Fierce-fanged, curve-clawed, rasp-tongued happy life.

I woke, as from a long limbo.
So the tins of catfood I bought from the shop were
        an anchor of sorts,
Stopped me from drifting away in my sterile sublime.

Now
She has me, the strawberry blonde
Who crosses her nose with her paws if I try to kiss it,
Or sits, sometimes, a Buddha, on the couch,
Paws folded neatly below,
Suffering my kisses planted on her nose with a
        saintly tolerance,
Turning her head just a little to the side,
Eyes closed and upslanting;

Who licks my beard with the rasp of her tongue if I
      catch her in a grooming frenzy,
Who leaps to my chest and places a single and
      talonless pad on my lips
If I whistle, who, if I open the door here at night as
      she sits in the chair
And walk down the path with the door left open,
      follows —
I see, looking back, her small head turned
Round the door edge, peering;
'Where are you going without me?' her look implies;
She cannot resist the magnetic night.

Mornings, when she squeezes somehow through the
      left-ajar window, over the sink in the kitchen,
And her ears spring up as they clear the pane-rim,
Her forepaws hooked on the window's edge, her
      hind legs clawing for purchase on the pane
      outside,
Just at the point when she's stuck half out, half-in,
I kiss her on the nose when she is most helpless,
And laugh, yet realise too, with the strange wild
      gleam in her eye as she comes in,
How that must seem to a bird in a tree hole,
As if the kitchen here were a giant tree-hole, and
      she coming in with me as her prey...

She arrives in my forest of books from the wood's
      university;
I lift her, sniffing wet mud on her paws from the
      miles of night-fields;
Counties of leafage upflourish in my mind when I sniff
      her fur,
Which, lustrously white on her paws, with a pale-gold
      tinge,
Is exactly like that on the old seed heads
      of the Spear Thistle
In forgotten corners of September fields.

Now the neighbours smile as they pass, at my
      accepting time.

She follows me out when I go to the tap on this hill
      for water,
At a certain speed in her walk her tail stands up
      with a little crook at the tip,
Or she'll be in spirited mood, bouncing about on
      her flexible spine; a strange thing,
She alone
(As we all are alone in the end), sistered by shadow,
Leaping in gaiety in the light of the catless moon.

Cunninghamhead Estate

Thirteen Ways
Of Looking at Edwin Morgan

I

Among twenty High Rises,
The main moving thing
Was the point of Eddie's pencil.

II

Stevens was of three minds. Eddie's
Is like a tree
In which there are three blackbirds,
Half a dozen Glasgow speugs,
A stuckie mimicking everything in sight,
Rooks loud at their nesting labours,
A scatter of linties and brichties and Pollokshield
    gowdspinks,
Three Steller's Sea Eagles, a Quetzal, a Kakapo,
The whirring glitter of a dozen bee hummingbirds,
Three species yet to be officially discovered,
And the last *Archaeopteryx lithographica*.

III

Eddie stood firm among the swaying Scottish bards.
He was a sane part of the pantomime.

IV

A young man and Eddie
Are one.

A young man and a pencil and Eddie
Are epic.

V

I do not know which to prefer:
The hammered
Craft of Eddie's sonnets
Or the gaiety of his experiments,
The long tradition
Or just after.

VI

Hailstones blatted the window
With strawberry-sized glass.
The shadow of Eddie
Crossed it, to and fro.
The mood
Was unlike that
In his poem of long ago.

VII

O wee men of Easterhouse,
Why do you imagine knives and scrotums?
Do you not see how Eddie
Is blasting off
To Saturn and Jupiter?

VIII

I know blind old men like Christ,
And what the sperm and egg might say;
And I know, too,
That Eddie is involved
In what I know.

IX

When Eddie soared out of sight
It marked a crick
In the necks of some contemporaries.

X

At the sound of Eddie
Reading his 'Loch Ness Monster Song',
Even the scholars of gravity
Would levitate slightly.

XI

He rode over Lanarkshire
On a glass Suzuki 1000.
Once, he experienced trepidation,
In that he mistook
The shadow of his motorbike
For Eddie's Concorde.

XII

The sun is shining.
Eddie must be writing.

XIII

It was night-time all day long.
It was dreich
And it was going to dreichen.
Eddie made light
With his pencil point.

Glasgow Vignettes

City of ease and possibilities —
Where after my quarter of a century's
Tramping the country roads
The nearest post-box was one minute's walk,
And milk forgotten did not require a new expedition.

City of blades and wrong looks,
Though not for me; of quirky encounters,
Where I passed a woman in heels and mini
In a downpour in Pollokshaws road
At two a.m. in December —
"Ony chance o yer brollie fer a lady, Mr?"
And I gave her mine, of course, nor even asked for a kiss,
And went dripping away down the road, and up the
            tenement stairs.

Where the view from my upper window
Was the lit rectangles of other lives in the early dark,
Lights turned off, turned on,
As frost crystallised on the tussocked gardens —
A student opposite, readying for his night out,
Combing his hair, dancing alone to his unheard music;
Gatherings of couples, wine and candles,
The memorable occasion
When a young Asian woman
Stripped at her pane to the buff with inviting gestures
As I sat hypnotised at my lettered table —
That window never looked the same again.
(I checked, often.)

City where one falls in love
Ten times a day, at least, or twenty,
And out again as quickly,
Where Sauchiehall Street in hot July
Is a long hallelujah of vivid women.

City of unexpected nature —
Goldfinches in birches at Pollokshields East
Not twittering in Glasgow accents, city
Where the starling that squealed
Over Buchanan Street's *Frasers*
Raised my eyes to a sparrowhawk's flight
Clutching the bird
Above heads of oblivious shoppers;
I stopped, to see it alight on a parapet, laser a yellow glare
Down at the carriered crowds
(While the wings flapped under its talons)
Then lift over roofs, to the starling's doom.

City of the glorious waitress of *Moyra Jane's*,
Wholesome as new baked bread,
Her finger as yet unringed,
Before the life she will step into
Dazzling the men,
Her due.

And of Central Station at six p.m. on a winter Friday,
That's a computer online, the people impulses
Charging the circuits, or that's a heart that these
Throngs rush through like corpuscles in blood
Feeding the flesh
Of hearths and bars, dances, courtships,
The solid marriages, illicit meetings, doomed romances,
And chill extremities.

Candles

I like their sheer simplicity —
wick and tallow,
the plain
white
or the perfumed
towers. So
sensitive too
their flames
that flicker and gutter in phantom gusts
like the spirit of quiet girls
before the opinionated,
the same spirit that eases
the mind coiled
to a too-tight spring.
To that doomed poet their light,
seeming too mellow, made
them liars akin to the moon —
to me they're plain exemplars
only of a different truth:
desire
in the blacked-out house.

They retain their power to touch the heart
among the computers and tinsel,
the holy primitives, being
as bare and calm as the thought of the soul.
Kin to the fire in the hearth, and small
cousin of the curious sun in the air,
lit by a common principle.

Put out the light of modernity.
Now, with a cupped match
kindling your features
bent to a wick,
you are like God
in the dark universe of this room.

The Minister of Air

(Epitaph on headstone, Ayr's Auld Kirk)
for Annie Lennox

I'm the minister of air,
And I've no care,
A sleepy sculptor's error
Saved me from his terror
  Of underground.

In the vertical miles up here
I gallop or poise, quite clear;
I lounge in the light's bounty
Above the whole spring county
  Shining round.

I'm the minister of air,
Not of lips or bone or hair:
No taut nets of the flesh
Catch me in their mesh —
  I'm free as rays.

I sparkle about you now,
The rustler of the bough,
The vessel for that star
Whose blistering fires you are —
  And envier of your days.

The Thought of Snow

The thought of snow,
　　At least, I like, because —
Despite what it makes
　　Of the world below
(Or that world makes of it) — it starts
　　With the aim of perfection:

　　Building itself to a lattice of white
On every mote of dust
　　Miles above, in cold —
Though it dies in disgrace in the streets of towns:
　　A tramp who had known big ideas,
A genuine artist, once,
　　A wasted prodigy, but beginning well.

Frost

-19.8°C.

My boots crunched on the frozen snow
that skinkled in the moonlight's glow,
and chill Orion glittered bright
across the south all Tuesday night,
while kitchen milk was tall and hard
and cooking oil congealed to lard
in the grimy unwashed frying pan
when I stepped into my caravan
in seventeen degrees below.
Frost ferns upon the dark window
splashed brashly as the work of some
mad graffitti artist. Numb,
I closed the door on stars and lit
the fire to thaw out, bit by bit,
was partly fascinated by
sheer cold that plummeted from the sky,
the slow relentless alchemy
that made, for instance, one from three:
knives in water in a cup
by their handles could be lifted up,
the whole swung round my head. Like rock,
my cat's food was a solid block
she could not eat, but only lick,
the cistern's water was clear brick,
my copper beard was well-spiculed
by crystals that my own breath fuelled,
out on the road, below barbed stars,
where hard-packed white slowed eager cars
moving like denizens. And no
technology could remove the snow

from miles of deathly country round
suffering cold without a sound,
its coal tits, finches, thrushes,
in holes in trees, in ivied bushes,
pitting against the space-frost night
their small hot hearts. Life was a fight
for warmth: gas, electric heaters, on,
were minor buttress to that one
sky-wide tower of cold above the roof
that kept as its slow-killing proof
the drops of glass from my each pane's
top inside sill, just like the lanes'
forged drops on hedge-thorns, universe
a stopped clock, the spacious hearse
of lips and laughter, and yet worse:
for death won't lock the Annick's flow
solid in chill where no winds blow,
and no clouds move, and no drops fall,
and the dull white shackles all.

On Wednesday, my sink's drain froze.
Each morning when I rose
I lifted the sink's ice-plate and threw
it out the door below the blue
tall lung-rasping air, then filled
my kettle with the single flow not stilled
to ice, up in the washhouse. The still
far moors, each treeless northward hill,
were stark-white streaked with black.
The wrecked sun barely rose till it sank back.
Again the dark, and Scotland caught
in cold negating every thought,
but one, and me, existing with my cat

who leapt in from the night and sat
beatific, eyes closed, before the fire.
We huddled in our matched desire,
for cold makes every level one
with its huge press, is paragon
of hopelessness — made cat, me,
coal tit, worm, alike in misery.

Each night before I went to bed
I warmed my bedroom with the red
bar of the electric fire,
melting the frost that in the higher
temperatures was damp unseen
unlike the mouldering black and green
along the west-faced wall. I crept
completely below cold covers, slept
(under ten blankets and a sheet)
curved like a broad bean and my feet
drawn up. I'd wake to panes
steel-ferned at eight, Kathleen Raine's
Living With Mystery, by my bed,
ironic, when I stuck my head
tentatively from my cave,
in minus seventeen, the grave
of grey-blue dawn. And then up,
to frost-stiff bread, a steaming cup
of tea, relentless day again;
and no desire to lift a pen,
but purely for the end of cold
impossible to praise, just tholed.

On Friday night an east wind rose
that still knifed through me, dripped my nose,
yet was a stirring of a kind
as I trudged home — the town behind
me, frost-crust, grimaces. That night
a bubble broke in the grim sight
of my sink's gravid water, then
settled to silence once again
for half an hour; and 'plopped' once more,
to settle silent as before.
The drain suddenly spluttered; dank
food-particled grimy water sank
back down to greasy steel, and flowed
away. I polished, till it glowed,
that stainless steel, I tidied up,
I drank tea as a ritual cup,
lard clarified in my frying pan,
the great clock of the universe began
ticking, and clouds occluded the
stars' glinting cold machinery.
Then rising was to shabby day
welcome, despite its drublie gray,
and my breath streaming on the glass.
Among the snow each patch of grass
swabbed green into the mind like spring,
the air relaxed, and everything
looked kinder out: water flowed
from guttering and the tyre-tracked road,
through Ayrshire and the counties round
Atlantic fragments splashed the ground
from billions of twigs. The frost's
vast stilled blue-grey vaults had lost

their ice-locks, and I felt my mind
relaxing again before the kind
wet westerlies, and aspirations re-
kindle like a May-sprung tree.
I saw folk in the sludge-brown towns
less hunched below their heavy frowns
relaxing into lifted eyes
and nods, and smiles, and enterprise;
the world like some great woken brain
birred with surprising thoughts again
where ice-drops melted and fused seeds
sat ready in earth like certain deeds.

The Holder-out

He sat in the palace of spectacular squalor,
A king, at least, of that small domain:
In the breeze-blocked hovel, misery's scholar
Drank mug after mug to toast his reign.

His cheeks were a disused-postbox red.
Light could not ease its letters through his eyes.
Whatever he'd held out for lay as dead
As the mouse the cat brought in and the littered flies.

It set for crown on him, poor king,
Tall gulfs of air through the grimy window,
And old crofts opened to an absolute thing:
Its rains rain and its long winds blow.

Orkney

Two Walks on Arthur's Seat

I

So you go up the Volunteer's Walk,
you rise with steepening ground
from the city's pubs and offices,
in a world of gorse and geology
enter an ancienter planet.

Fading of city's sound.
See the gorse? — rich perfume of coconut, its
million gold wicks lit by the heightening sun.
It'll be hoaching with nests...

Dozens of finches' breasts — linnets and redpolls —
pressed to their eggs, hidden
deep in these yellow seas of thorns.
To them the city below is nothing,
irrelevance, passing. They are on older business.
Hour by hour the frail
Embryos add to themselves: skull, beak, claw,
in the snug dark, waiting
to burst into light that is everything.

We sit on the edge of a crag overlooking the valley.
Below, the notes of birds:
                    There, a whitethroat —
that desultory rush of song;
                    the creak of pipits;
there, a willow warbler's
                    frail diminuendo,

like the twirling fall of a tiny petal, and
a song thrush
                up on the slope behind us, playing
his flute,
  his flute,
    his flute,
      his flute.

Can that be a skylark? —
                 it is —
a rare bird now,
light as an envelope
              twittering
                  invisibly
in miles of vertical air,
               a miniature, dark
defender of skylark hopes.

Somewhere,
under a tussock,
his mate will sit on her nest
of dried and delicate grasses.

One feels an intruder, almost,
among this fundamental
seriousness of earth.

I would like to find you a nest, a minor act
of surrogate veneration
among such birth and breeding.
At fifteen I'd have found twenty by now,
though I had no woman acquaintance, then,
who would have liked to be shown one.

Here, at forty two,
it's nests that are hard to come upon.

I bend the same, look up
among the riot of thorns,
keep out a weather eye
for the especial sprigs
that, jostled, once produced
the sudden small-winged burst,
the stiff brief whirr of feathers...
Then the forward rush,
parting the sprays —
                              a linnet's!, say,
with six eggs in it, white,
                              speckled, hot
in the round cup lined with the hair of horses...

But not today!
Though a cock bullfinch,
dandy of carmine breast and black,
appears from a tuft of gorse, as if
from some magician's hat...
"Ah ha!" I say, "a nest!"
But nothing. Punctuating gorse.
I come out,
like a dog shaking off water
shake off a little shower
of twigs and thorns and yellow petals.

We go on, up, up
in the stillness
the pulses knocking in our necks,
past an American saying

"My favourite place on earth..."
and sit on an outcrop, over
Duddingston Loch.
                            Space and air.
A mute swan's
                    speck of white
broods, serene
among the reed beds at the loch's far end.
Beauty presiding
over the rabble coots.

The faintest breeze
arriving from over the Pentlands
across its miles of air
trembles a thousand
tormentil blossoms,
lifts our hair;
a wheatear, fresh from Africa,
flirts its white/black tail,
with a flick and a flurry
flits in fear
always a little ahead
as we descend the printed track
back to our current century;

ahead the hundred thousand
minds of the city, doors
opening, closing, pints
rising and falling,
arguments, fall outs, kisses, smiles,
the miles of city streets,
glitter of wedding rings in the jewellers' windows,
the beeping terminals...

Behind us, the rocks are calm,
the finches nest in the yellow gorse.

II

This morning I'm alone.
     Big day,
dark clouds billow
up over crag and buttress,
wrestle the sun; tiny human silhouettes
catch the eye
    on stone skylines.
The wind
    is blowing everything one way —
cocksfoot grasses, burnt out, lashing their heads,
the gliding clouds
that switch off the sun like a lightbulb.
Then sun-blaze,
     panning across the slopes, startling
grass to emerald,
    buffing
two crows off crags in mid-air
cawing, "caa-caa-caa!", dipping and rising,
the black plumage grazed
     to saw-sheared metals.

The gorse has sputtered out.
Not a yellow blossom anywhere,
May's masses
doused by autumn.

Easy, here, to find yourself alone.
Only the wind, riffling in your ears,

that materialises
like a dark familiar
                    on the panicky grass
your stretched shadow.
Jostlework of cumuli, gray,
the lightshot castellations,
tumbling away
over the hills to the Pentlands...

I sit on the same mossed crag as once in spring.

Now the wind rages,
it cannot bear that things be kept —
records, notes,
                    it wants to rip the pages
out of the notebook fluttering
like a leg-trapped linnet, and send them
                              miles into the Firth.
It buffets so hard up here
my script on the page
is the feet of a wandering spider
dipped in ink.

Across the valley
two birch saplings,
                    lissom as girls, gesticulate
in the wind,
are backlit
            by the sun;
while the slope
        on which they stand
is shadow, they .
                    glitter in particular

green and yellow
                    their lucent sequins —
candelabra of lit leaves...
a cloud
            covers the sun;
the birches
blown out, as by a breath.

I push up, against gravity,
heart-thud, gusts,
on my left hand,
                    slowly expanding, the wide
sweep of Firth,
            cloud daubs, a shower
dragging its smeared pearls out
over the sea
from the houses crammed at the coastline —
among gray cumuli
one whose tall top's brilliant white on blue,
a soprano among the basses,
                    the bride among dark suits
startling the eye...

A wee boy asks his father, "Can you see our house?"

Up at the summit, no
roar of magma now,
                    only the thunderous wind,
the view, breathtaking,
I at the centre of a clock-face
                    round its far perimeter
from one o'clock to four
                    hills

Largo Law
    Kellie Law
        The Isle of May's faint smudge through binoculars
           and the Bass Rock's buttress
             North Berwick Law
                the autumn patchwork
at the foot of the Lammermuirs,
the Firth blue-skied,
           crowded with lit cumuli...

At nine o'clock,
      down there
          over the jewelled
circuitry of the city
         sweeps of black, squalls
rush in from over the Pentlands at my back —
such visible weathers!
Sudden dusk
      in the city —
I imagine
the big drops
       bouncing off streets,
sprouting of instant umbrellas,
           frowns,
the sprinting for shelter,
         the rattling
on the streaming office panes,
folk saying:
      "Look at the day out there!"

While the ships on the Firth
shine
in the light

and the Lammermuirs' fields are lambent green and gold.

Here
I grasp the triangulation point
not to be blown away,
                    start back down
try to outpace
                like a wheatear
before the walker,
                    the rain advancing...
Till it begins,
            thudding
into the hills,
                rattling my anorak hood,
spattering Duddingston Loch,

amazingly leaving unsoaked

the plumes of its dipping Swans...

Raw cold
a harsher world
                reddens my hands
as I squelch
back down the track
with the summit stragglers,

to civil warmth
and a new pint's tangy gold.

Prism

i.m. George Mackay Brown

The tall bright arch on the black cloud —
As the squall rushes the islands,

Rattling the panes, grimacing women and men —
As the vast cloud speeds off over the sea,

Fades; and the clear light blazes round.
The seven hues die to the sun again.

From: SpeyGrian Venture

for Joyce Gilbert

I

In the time of the image, from the place of mirrors
(where I leave a thread so as not to be lost)
I came to the Spey with a jaded mind, out of the cities of
      glamour.
Seeking like others I don't know what
but hoping those waters would rinse the images out of the
      cells of my brain,
as when I was little I'd count up to ten and say when I
      reached it
"All that I do from now on will be graceful",
I hope for the Spey to cleanse me anew.

II

At the house for the wild birds at the Insh marshes,
a brilliant Sunday, we gather in Cairngorm quiet
for introductions out on the lawn. A half-forgotten
room in my mind, dusty with years of neglect
opens at the sound of redpolls high overhead
and lets in the light and a bit of breeze. Our tents are
      pitched
overlooking bog cotton and asphodel sprinkled below in
      the marshes;
snipe
"tchicking" and "tchacking" nightlong soon
mingle with snores, as the tents make a small archipelago
of snoring and silent islands, under the partial moon.

III

It is good to have nothing to do but dismantle the tent,
it is good to notice the long-tailed tits by their calls like
    little
lengths of beads in a stand of birches,
and to have heard through night and morning the
    "bleating"
courtship flight of the snipe, a speck somewhere in the sky,
its stiff tail feathers vibrating as it dives at the earth.
It is good to hear there are buzzards somewhere, invisible,
from their cries in the cells of your brain.
(Once in a lane at Cunninghamhead a grasshopper
    warbler
sang for a month and I thought it a fair bet no one
else even noticed its song or in any event would have known
what it was if they did, as it sang for a mate there.)
It is good to marry a warbler's song and its name,
and to be back in a place where the calls of birds
are abundant, far out of the cities of style.

V

The long slow paddle across Loch Insh, and its black
    waters.
Before we enter the head of the Spey we pause in front of
    the osprey's
nest in a pine on its island, to the well-grown young's
    repeated alarm,
echoing, brassy. Barely a mile further down there's the adult
on the topmost bough of a Scots pine, perching like a
    film star,
showing its jagged nape feathers, as we drift below.

I notice as much how a common sandpiper twinkles,
  bobbing,
along the length of a bough horizontal over the river,
then up a vertical branch delicately picks its way —
neat as an epigram, to the sonnet of the osprey.

VI

The commonest birds of the Spey —

the grey
wagtail,
its sulphur yellow
dazzling its name
like sudden sun on a dreich day,
and that will line the old
nest of a blackbird
for the clutch of frail-shelled gold
preciouser than metal;

the heron,
fish spear on a rope of feathers, cheeringly
lugubrious, straggly-crested,
flapping away with the grave
deliberation of an undertaker
ahead of our line
of canoes;

sandmartins' chirring colonies
occupy the banks,
but those savings will fly to Africa
and the bank manager's the sun;

redshanks, peewits, curlews,
and the sleek red-breasted merganser
flickering away downstream
with its white wing patches
flashing, and the panicked, aquaplaning
flotillas of mallard ducklings
ploughing deep furrows of water,
wobbling from side to side away,
each with a miniature pipe
stuck in its throat.

If the Spey is a fluid sentence,
these are its punctuation,
if it's a clarsach of water
these are the lightest tunes
the creation plays on its strings...

From: **A Day at Lawthorn Primary**

III

Outside, too, there is lots going on:
In a pool in Lawthorn Wood,
While Stacey is dotting her "i"s
And Stuart is thinking and thinking
And Laura is tranquilly writing
And Kayleigh is asking again
If she can keep the old nest of a song thrush,
The small black dots of the frogspawn
Are dreaming themselves into tadpoles, tadpoles, tadpoles,
Though they will never survive
For the daft frogs hadn't a care
That the standing water would dry up in days,
Though still the dying frogspawn dreams
Between the old cans and the rotting logs
Of its world of a million frogs of a beautiful green,
For that is the way of nature. And the daftness of these
      amphibians
Is hardly the fault of the sun.

And all of the birds are singing at Lawthorn,
Song Thrush, Blackbird, Robin and Wren
Sing their songs and sing them again,
Great Tit, Blue Tit, Chaffinch and Chiffchaff
Sing and flirt and if birds could laugh
These would be laughing for feathery joy
In the sunlit morning. Goldfinch, Goldcrest,
Long-tailed Tit and the odd Treecreeper
That jerks up the trunks of trees like a little woodpecker
With a sharp curved beak in its search for spiders,

All of them sing and think of their nest
Full of hot eggs and each feathery breast
Pressed to the living ovals.
                              It is light that makes this happen:
If the sun is a great composer,
Light is the great conductor
Dancing to various musics this May
Ceilidh out of the secret throats of the birds...

Think of the worms in their hundreds of thousands,
Pink butcher meat underground for the birds and moles
While, up above, the children jink and argue and reel
In the shining air with the white clouds
Stately and slowly changing their shapes on the skylines
And the sun is a flash in the blue.
                              But is that the bell?
Jangling time makes its commands.
The children line up, the teacups
Are rinsed and set on the draining board in the staffroom;
A kind of calm, and the learning, begin again.

What is the capital of China?
How do you spell surrender?
How many wings has a dragonfly?
Did anyone here have a granddad who worked as a miner?

Mrs MacLean, can I go to the toilet?
Mrs MacLean, I've got a skelf in my finger!
Mrs MacLean, Willie McCrackle keeps kicking me!

The class's energy
Is like a saucepan of milk about to boil over its rim
Till a few skilled words from the teacher
Turns down the gas to a peep.

Outside the weather is starting to alter, the sunlight
That jewels the desks of classrooms fades;
And a breeze, rising, moves through the new-leafed trees
Of Lawthorn Wood. A million leaves of fresh frail lime
Tremble in tops of the trees and the massive
      skies of Ayrshire
Darken. But you'd have to be the Sparrowhawk
That, at 11.25 am, is circling high over Lawthorn rooftops
And its classes of learning and scribbling and talk,
To see the sun shining still on the peaks of Arran
And the hills of the Fairlie Moors. Up at this height
Lawthorn Primary's cars are merest matchbox toys
And the wind in the silence ruffles the hawk's barred
      feathers.
The world below is spread out to its marvellous eyesight
Like a stunningly-detailed photograph.
It could probably make out the words in the open jotters,
This ambushing killer that likes small birds — Chiffchaff,
Blue Tit, Blackbird, Song Thrush, swoops
Up over hedges and explodes with a rush
Of talons and hooked beak into a small bird's world.

It's lunchtime, lunchtime, stomachs are rumbling and
      the dining hall
Is filled with the succulent smells
Of roast potatoes, sausages, macaroni cheese and chips,
The hotplates are winking their chrome, the kind dinner
      ladies
Smilingly serve up the food of the earth
For food is joy, and each girl and boy
Twitters like a finch at the airy tables
Or waits in the straggling queue.

High in the wind-swayed wood
That sounds like a sea and creaks
Like the deck and the rigging
Of a clipper (where is that old ship sailing to?)
The Sparrowhawk's grip
Is tight round the neck of a Blackbird.
The blade like a butcher's aimed by the lasering eyes
Hacks to the glistening red
And down and feathers drift and blow through the
      wood.
A hen Blackbird is suddenly a widow, but a Long-tailed Tit
Gathers a beakful of the black plumes
To line its nest — which in time may be filled with two
      thousand feathers,
Then a dozen pure white and red-peppered eggs, not much
      bigger than marrowfat peas —
A cradle-coffin, up in the creaking boughs.

Vision

The gale rose in the night and as we lay
Soon I at least was restive as that air,
Though you slept quietly on. I turned in dark,
Hearing the bare trees' roar a field away,
And then the oorie calm before each next
Gust hit from across the miles. I had to rise
Eventually; opened the kitchen door and put
My head out in the Universe, to sheer
Spacious night, where the clouds had blown
To wisps and scraps across the face of stars
Scattered above the world, as wind roared here;
Seeing the Plough as I had rarely known it,
Upside down, and strange stars in the sky,
Autumn's familiars set, although the Pleiades
Were glittering far and tinily
Up in a windy gallery of the West.

Two things had fought and one had won,
So anything it seemed might happen then.
I didn't want to be the only one to see,
So came back in and went at last to bed.
I could hardly say that I was happy
At those gusts draughting through
The vast wrecked house of the world,
With no one likely to build that house again.

The News of Swans

Bad tempered, hot, I cleared the rise
With two wet miles on foot ahead;
Wind-buffeted, and soaked by skies,
"The meek will inherit the Earth!" I said.
Though maybe that was true enough,
It wasn't in a tone of truth I said it:
The rains too wet and winds too rough
For such old tales to be given credit.

Then, on my dark sight, a vision gleamed —
Seventeen swans on the flooded pool! —
At least in the dreich that's what they seemed
With their aura of being beyond our rule,
Their aura of being beyond our lies.
Nor at my passing did they scare,
But flapped their wings and made small cries.
They could not be soaked by the soaking air.

I almost threw my umbrella away —
My portable heaven — but not quite,
So happy I grew in the lashing day
At seeing that marriage of bird and light.
The following morning of course they were gone
To some further place, like a startling news:
The floodpool was empty where they had shone —
And more ragged and worn my clothes and shoes.

The Overtoun Road

Notes on the Poems

16: W. B. Yeats met Maud Gonne in 1899 and courted her for over fifteen years, before marrying Georgie Hyde-Lees in 1917. Yeats and Gonne conducted a sizeable correspondence, but the relationship may have been unconsummated apart from on one occasion, reputedly in 1908.

17: The "comb" in line 3 refers to the comb-like design of the leading edge of the first primary feather in an owl's wing, which serves to soften the air flow over the wing, and aids silent flight.

20: "Overtoun": the Overtoun road, some two miles long, runs from near Cunninghamhead Estate to Springside in Ayrshire. I walked it literally thousands of times in 25 years.

25: "nidifugous" refers to the young of birds able to look after themselves within hours of hatching, such as those of gulls and waders. "Nidicolous" refers to chicks which are entirely helpless at birth and have to be fed by the parents, though the chicks usually grow rapidly, in a matter of 12-16 days. All passerines fall into this category.

The Heron's "pectinated claw" consists of a row of little notches on one of the claws of the bird's foot; if covered in slime after feeding on, say, an eel, the bird mixes powder from special feathers on its breast with the slime, then combs it off using this claw.

"*Strix aluco*": the Tawny Owl.

30: "Lady's-smock": also known as Cuckoo Flower, a crucifer with lilac blossom, common in May.

A different individual is addressed in each of these sonnets.

34-35: This poem is my response as part of a good-natured spat with the Scottish poet David Kinloch, whose sestina, 'Braveheart', makes swingeing reference to "the land of villanelles and sonnets"; I took this, in part — and correctly as it turned out — as a sideswipe at *The Dark Horse*, the Scottish-American poetry magazine I edit. In its early days, particularly, it was a strong advocate for metre and rhyme in poetry. It has since relaxed its approach.

'Braveheart' appears on pp 74-75 of Kinloch's recent collection *Un Tour d'Ecosse* (Carcanet, 2001).

39: "Emily": Emily Dickinson, whom the narrator of this poem seems to imagine — surely erroneously — as something of a shrinking violet.

42: Among a page of advertisements for butchers' shops and 30th birthday celebrations, this notice appeared in *The Arran Banner*.

48: "the class": the school was Irvine Royal Academy. The Waxwing is a handsome bird about the size of a starling, an irregular winter visitor to Britain, found only when food shortages in its native Scandinavia and north Russia lead to periodic waxwing "irruptions". The bird often visits suburban gardens, where it feeds on cotoneaster berries.

53: One of the largest colonies of Arctic terns in Europe nests at the North Hill, an RSPB nature reserve, on Papa Westray. Summer visitors, the terns leave the islands very suddenly — almost overnight.

"When I went out for water...": at Cunninghamhead Estate in Ayrshire, where this poem was written, I had no plumbed water for twelve years. Water came from an outside tap.

54: "Warwickdale Hill": the highest point on the Overtoun Road.

56-61: Papa Westray is one of the smallest of the inhabited Orkney islands at some four miles long and around a mile across at its widest point. Tom Mackay, one of the island's true "characters" (he had never been out of the islands in 70 years) died in his bed there in the late 1990s. Stewart Groat was the subject of my poem "Islander," in my first book of poems, *The Shell House*.

62: Fairliecrevoch was originally a farm, the farmhouse of which was later redeveloped as flats and the land sold to surrounding farmers. It lies about half a mile from Cunninghamhead Estate, across the local river, the Annick Water.

64: "Beretta": an Italian shotgun. P. Beretta, near Milan, is one of the world's leading makers of sporting firearms.

66: Eight minutes is a close approximation. In fact, sunlight takes a further 20 seconds to reach earth.

67: Fieldfares and Redwings are species of thrush from northern Europe which winter here. The Fieldfare has a characteristic "chack-chack-chack" call; the Redwing, a single high pitched "seep!" The birds occur in large flocks and can often be heard on winter nights.

70: The Lesser Redpoll is a delicate little finch just over four inches long, with a red forehead.
    "herrying": pillaging, pilfering.

72: Timothy Murphy is a pig farmer, venture capitalist, and poet of the plain style from North Dakota. His poem 'Sunset at the Getty' imagines that Californian institution wrecked by earthquake. It was published in *The Dark Horse*, issue 2, p.10, Autumn 1995.

73: "larach": ruined building.

75: Roy Campbell (1902-57) published this poem in his collection *Adamastor* (1931). The opening stanza reads:

> I love to see, when leaves depart,
> The clear anatomy arrive,
> Winter, the paragon of art,
> That kills all form of life and feeling
> Save what is pure and will survive.

76: Hugh MacDiarmid's former home, Brownsbank Cottage, near Biggar in South Lanarkshire, is now a base for a writer-in-residence. I lived there from September 1997-September 1999. MacDiarmid's lyric 'The Little White Rose' is inscribed on a paving stone at the cottage's door. 'The Eemis Stane' is an early MacDiarmid lyric in Scots which deals with the insignificance of human life "among the infinities".

77: "greeshoch": embers.
    "bent-frail": a "bent" is a grass stalk.

78: MacDiarmid was reputed to use the white shed behind Brownsbank cottage for writing in. I found it too cold in winter and too hot in summer.

79: MacDiarmid's wife, Valda Trevlyn, dyed her hair red until her death at the age of 83.

84: "speugs": sparrows; "stuckie": starling; "linties": linnets; "brichties": chaffinches; "gowdspinks": goldfinches. Steller's Sea Eagle is the world's largest eagle, found in remote parts of Russia. The German nature photographer Klaus Nigge estimated that the nest of one pair he photographed in Kamchatka would have been large enough to accommodate a double bed. The male Quetzal is a dazzling emerald bird with a tail that can be up to three feet long. It is found in the montane forests of central America. The Kakapo of New Zealand, flightless, nocturnal, is the largest, rarest parrot on earth. *Archaoepteryx lithographica* is a famous fossil first discovered in the Solnhofen area of Germany in 1861. It is reputed to be the "missing link" in the evolution of birds from reptiles.

88: After leaving Brownsbank Cottage in September 1999, I spent a winter in Pollokshields, on Glasgow's south side. I had never experienced the amenities of city life before.

92: "Air": variant spellings of names were formerly common, though it's amusing to imagine this one as wishful thinking. Annie Lennox is a professional photographer and the wife of the American poet-critic David Mason.

93: Each snow crystal, which in agglomerations form snowflakes, needs a substrate as a pearl needs a sandgrain — in the snow crystal's case, the dust particles floating in billions in the atmosphere.

94: Christmas Day to 29 December, 1995, recorded some of the lowest temperatures in Scotland last century. Many people died in various cold-related circumstances.

100-108: This poem was commissioned by the performing artist Anne-Marie Culhane for a lottery-funded project "Exploring Place" using Arthur's Seat in Edinburgh.

Numerous photographers, visual artists and writers were involved. My first walk was on 25 May, 2001. My second, on 15 October , 2001.

110-113: "SpeyGrian" is the working title for a group of artists, writers, scientists and musicians gathered by the scientist Dr Joyce Gilbert to develop new ways of integrating the sciences and the arts. The group was set up in mid-2000 and, from 25 June to 1 July of that year, 19 individuals canoed the length of the Spey, putting in at Ruthven Barracks near the Insh Marshes, and camping nightly at various pre-arranged sites en route. Part of the expected "outcome" was artwork, prose or verse about the experience. I print here the five sections of my 12-part poem which I hope transcend their occasion.

111: The Grasshopper Warbler, a small brown bird around five inches long, is rarely seen as it loves skulking around in undergrowth. Its presence can only be verified by the male's song: a queer, continuous chirring note, like the whirring of a tiny machine, rising and falling in pitch.

114-117: This is an excerpt from a poem of over 600 lines written during a Public Arts Residency I held between March and June 2002 at Lawthorn Primary School, North Ayrshire, under the management of Linda Mallett (Public Arts Officer, NAC),with the co-operation of Elizabeth McKendrick, head teacher. The poem grew from a series of writing/nature workshops with one P6 class, linking the school to the adjoining grounds. Other sections of the piece include a collaboration with the children, incorporating lines and phrases written by them. The piece will soon be published as a pamphlet, with artwork by the class, available from me: gjctdh@freenetname.co.uk

119: The species in this poem is the Whooper Swan. Though it's approximately the same size as its relative, the Mute Swan, it's identified by the yellow, not orange, on the beak, and its characteristic "honking" cries, strangely musical, like the sound of odd bells, when a group is gathered together. Additionally, while the Mute Swan is often associated with humans and may be semi-tame, the Whooper is genuinely wild. Whooper Swans are migratory, and winter in Britain from Scandinavia.

'Nothing but Heather!'

GERRY CAMBRIDGE
Scottish Nature in Poems, Photographs and Prose

SHORE CRAB

Haw, Jimmy, dinnae mess wi me.
Fancy yer chances, eh? Eh? We'll see.
Naw, they dinnae caw
me Shug the Claw
fer naethin. 'Mon, square go then.
    'Srang,
ye feart? Ahve taen a haill gang
o the likes o ye at wance.
Dinny reckon yer chance
noo, eh? When ye get tae hell
ah'll be waitin there fer ye. Caw
me a scroonger, eh? Aye, awa
an rin ti yer maw
ya wimp! Mind o Shug the Claw.

48 poems matched with 48 captioned photographs. In his introduction Cambridge explores the origins of the project, and the approaches to nature taken by other poets, and incorporates a wry account of an unwillingly-sectarian, bird-obsessed adolescence in rural Ayrshire in the 1970s.

"Cambridge is in the tradition of Scottish naturalists like Hugh Miller, John Muir and David Stephen... This book, a mix of entertainment and education, will delight..."
JAMES ROBERTSON, Scotland on Sunday

Luath Press Limited

committed to publishing well-written books worth reading

LUATH PRESS takes its name from Robert Burns, whose little collie Luath (*Gael.*, swift or nimble) tripped up Jean Armour at a wedding and gave him the chance to speak to the woman who was to be his wife and the abiding love of his life. Burns called one of *The Twa Dogs* Luath after Cuchullin's hunting dog in *Ossian's Fingal*. Luath Press grew up in the heart of Burns country, and now resides a few steps up the road from Burns' first lodgings on Edinburgh's Royal Mile. Luath offers you distinctive writing with a hint of unexpected pleasures.

Most bookshops in the UK and parts of Europe, the US, Canada, Australia and New Zealand either carry our books in stock or can order them for you. To order direct from us, please send a £sterling cheque, postal order, international money order or your credit card details (number, address of cardholder and expiry date) to us at the address below. Please add post and packing as follows: UK — £1.00 per delivery address; overseas surface mail — £2.50 per delivery address; overseas airmail — £3.50 for the first book to each delivery address, plus £1.00 for each additional book by airmail to the same address. If your order is a gift, we will happily enclose your card or message at no extra charge.

Luath   Press Limited
543/2 Castlehill
The Royal Mile
Edinburgh EH1 2ND
Scotland
Telephone: 0131 225 4326 (24 hours)
Fax: 0131 225 4324
e-mail: gavin.macdougall@luath.co.uk
Website: www.luath.co.uk